T0117112

Visit: www.Ravengeopolnews.com/ebooks

39 Years of Clinton Scandals and Corruptions 1997–2016 (Volume III of III)

Joseph P. Hawranek, Ph.D

Trafford rev. 05/14/2019

 www.trafford.com
North America & international
toll-free: 1 888 232 4444 (USA & Canada)
fax: 812 355 4082

CONTENTS

PART 1.   THE SERVER

PART 2.   THE CLINTON FUND

39 YEARS OF CLINTON SCANDALS AND CORRUPTION 1977 TO 2016

BOOK 3 of 3

CLINTON SERVER AND CLINTON FUND
Joseph P. Hawranek, PH.D.

The time has come to tell the truth about the corruption of the government employee unions in this country. - Newt Gingrich

Public corruption is the FBI's top criminal priority. The threat - which involves the corruption of local, state, and federally elected, appointed, or contracted officials - strikes at the heart of government, eroding public confidence and undermining the strength of our democracy. - James Comey

The government is so out of control. It is so bloated and infested with fraud, deceit, corruption, and abuse of power. Ted Nugent

In a state where corruption abound, laws must be very numerous - Tacitus

INTRODUCTION

This book will have two parts, Part 1 – The Server and Part 2 – The Clinton Fund.

PART 1 – THE SERVER

We will examine the controversy surrounding Hillary Clinton's private server. This notorious server was used throughout her tenure of Senator and Secretary of State. Her period of office was from January 21, 2009 to February 1, 2013.

The server was installed in her basement. It was not a secure server. It did not have firewalls, identification and pass word protection nor encryption. We do not know whether it had back up. Accordingly, it provided easy access for a sophisticated hackers and intelligence communities of large nations.

The server contained all emails, public and private, that Hillary used throughout her service as your as Secretary of State. It has now come out that this was 30,000 official business Emails and 31,000 private business Emails. Further, it must have contained all of the emails associated with the Clinton fund since Hillary's presidential campaign has been merged with the Clinton Foundation. During her administration, the Foundation grew to $600 million. Wikipedia now reports that has grown and is now $2 billion.

PART 2 – THE CLINTON FUND

The Clinton Foundation will be examined in Part two of this book. The press refers to the Foundation as a Fund so I will also. They are the same. This Charitable Foundation appears to be a means to hide the amount taken in donations, to pay no taxes, to hide the names of donors and to provide a slush fund for the Clintons. It is currently under FBI criminal investigation

We will examine the transaction that Secretary Clinton approved that gave ownership of 20% of U.S. Uranium Production to Russia.

We will also assess the amount of some of the money that went to the foundation.

THE AUTHOR'S SECURITY CREDENTIALS

I am a 40-year retiree from IBM. I worked as a manager as well as a System Engineer in several areas. For the last assignment before retirement, I worked as a Global Services Consultant. I am IBM certified as a Communications and Security Consultant in banking. My areas of specialization were Communications, Security and Business Resiliency. Business Resiliency refers to backups. I have IBM certified technical expertise in these disciplines.

HILLARY'S SERVER

In a normal industry or government environment for data processing, one should protect the computer system by using a firewall. The firewall is a convenient name for a system that requires one to ascertain communication inquiries into the system as a friend or a foe. As such, firewalls contain protection systems to keep out the active attacks and passive attacks on the system Active attacks are those that penetrate to do harm.

Passive attacks are those that penetrate to gather information and then leave. A number of techniques are used to protect the valuable assets in the data base resident on the server. Some are

- Identification of certain IP addresses as being dangerous.
- Verify Ids – Identification and Pass words
- Create encrypted data pathways between remote locations and the home server
- Encrypt critical information resident on the server

As far as I can tell by the information released thus far, none of this was accomplished for Hillary Clinton's PDAs, communications and her server... Physical security was provided since Secret Service agents are constantly available to Bill Clinton. They protect the residence because he is a former President.

Hillary violated every principle of security for protected assets. The assets in this instance were American top-secret, secret and confidential information held by the Secretary of State of this nation. This not only included state secrets but also contact information to informants as well as critical personnel in foreign governments.

Accordingly, it now appears, based on the information released, as if there was

- No firewall
- No encrypted data paths
- No encrypted data
- No record keeping as required by Federal regulations – a felony
- No adherence to good security practice for Personal Digital Assistants or laptops.
- Frequent use of unencrypted and insecure plain text PDAs in Russia, China and other possible non-friendly nations.

The use of the non-secure Blackberry phone is particularly significant because

- State Department Security specifically recommended against blackberry use in foreign lands in writing to Hillary. She replied, *"I get it."* Then she used them anyway.
- Blackberry PDAs can communicate local voices when off. To *"quiet"* them, one must remove the battery. This practice was not followed.
- All PDAs must transmit to the local tower and then the message is relayed forward to the end tower no matter where it is. Transmission to the first tower in unfriendly nations allows them to pick up the conversation in plain text and to "hear" the conversation in both directions. Remember, they provide the encrypted data path between the PDA and the tower. At the tower, it can be removed and the plain text is read. Nothing is confidential much less secret. This was the Hillary Clinton and her staff's normal practice.
- Any good intelligence agency – Russia and China are included here – would pick up the plain text and "hear" the conversation in both directions. It was like being on a TV stage

where everyone – including our adversaries – could listen to everything that was said.

SECURITY DELUSION

A common delusion by the non-technical person is that if the physical location of the server is safe, then the server is safe from intrusion. This is simply not true. The server communication lines are where the intruders attack. I have visited banks in New York where armed guards with 45 caliber weapons sit at the door and keep you from entering the data processing center. This keeps out the thugs from destroying the data center but it does not keep out the silent attacks that come about by means of hundreds of telephone lines terminating at the data center computers. This is where active and passive attacks occur – the communication network.

METHODOLOGY FOR PART 1 AND 2

My approach in **Part one, The Server**, is to proceed as follows:

- Federal Laws and Regulations: Explain what are the Federal Laws and Regulations that must be obeyed to be a responsible professional in the position of Secretary of State and not to commit a felony.
- Review what actually occurred
- Explain what was found by the FBI
- Postulate an explanation of the Justice Department's decisions
    o The AG to recuse herself
    o The FBI not to recommend indictment given that there were clear felony violations made.

In **Part 2, The Clinton Foundation,** I will review what I have found on the internet. Virtually nothing has been released that I can find on the donors who have donated to the fund. Some information is on the internet about the size of the Fund - $600 million at the time that Secretary Clinton left her office to today at $2 billion as reported by WikiLeaks.

I will explain how the Fund works and how it is used to dodge taxes and hide the donor names. Finally, I show how it could be used to extort hundreds of millions from foreign nationals for special "favors" from the Secretary of State. This allegation would have to be proved before I say it is a fact. In return for payments, the Secretary can give "approvals" for actions that would not normally be approved.

In this part, I will briefly review James Comey's background to highlight that multiple times in the past; he has appeared to let the Clintons be exonerated. I will specifically review his double standard on the government's requirement for control of classified information. Hillary went free after massive disregard for the law because she did not "intend" to do harm. Others did not get off indictments for minor violations. Finally, "intent" is not in the law. If you went through the stop sign, it is a felony.

I will postulate and briefly review what Comey may have been thinking if he was ordered to let Hillary go free by his political bosses – Lynch and Obama.

Upon completion, I will draw some conclusions. The FBI decision not to recommend that Hillary be indicted, when you review Hillary's actions and practices, is almost unbelievable. Trump is apparently correct, ***"The Fix is in."***

PART 1

THE SERVER

OFFICE OF INSPECTOR GENERAL (OIG)

The U.S. Department of State (DOS) has its own Inspector General. In in April 2015, the Office of Inspector General (OIG) initiated an evaluation to address concerns and to respond to requests from the current Secretary of State and members of Congress. [i]

Specifically, they were to investigate non-departmental systems and to conduct analysis of record preservation requirements associated with the Freedom of Information Act (FOIA) compliance. Judicial Watch, a private "watchdog" organization, had sent several FOIA compliance requests into the Department of State.

The OIG formally reviewed the requirements of the

- Federal Records Act (FRA)
- Federal Information Security Management Act (FISMA)
- Regulations required by the National Archives and Records Administration (NARA),
- Foreign Affairs, Manual (FAM) and the Foreign Affairs Handbook (FAH) that all DOS employees are expected to comply.

I will quote frequently from the law so that no misunderstanding occurs about what constitutes a felony if procedures are not followed.

The FRA requires that the head of each agency to

> *"Make and preserve records containing adequate and proper documentation of the organization, functions, policies, decisions, procedures, and* <u>*essential transactions*</u> *of the agency designed to furnish information necessary to protect the legal and financial rights of the government and of persons directly affected by the agency's activities."*

It was found that secretary Clinton did not meet the above requirement. Specifically, it found that -

> *"Secretary Clinton employed a personal email system to conduct business during her*

tenure in the United States Senate and her 2008 presidential campaign. She continued to use personal email throughout her term as secretary, relying on an account maintained on a private server, predominantly through mobile devices. Throughout Secretary Clinton's tenure, the server was located in her own New York residence."

Due to FOIA requests by Judicial Watch, the DOS formally asked Secretary Clinton for all emails associated with business at the Department of State after she left office on February 1, 2013. They had to sue a year later since she did not comply with department regulations by supplying all her business records when she left her office... She complied in December 2014 (22 months after leaving office) as follows:

- 55,000 hardcopy pages representing 30,000 emails associated with official business
- She kept 31,000 personal records that were selected from the existing 61,000 Emails. Her personal attorney without involvement of DOS did the selection. This violates law. Hillary by law, cannot legally remove the Emails after she left employment at DOS only before she left her employment at DOS. Because of this fact, all of the Server Emails were DOS property.
- She supplied a letter stating she had a practice of sending copies to State Department employees at their business location. Thus, she felt that this should provide adequate digital database documentation.

In summary, Secretary Clinton's position was that the department already had records of the secretary's email preserved within its record keeping systems. She was "stonewalling" her felonious practices. Delay is one of her most frequently used techniques.

In sharp contrast to the above performance, the government requirements for securing Emails have been consistent. The laws and policies since 1995 have been clear and never changed. Specifically –

- The FRA requires documentation of ***"essential transactions"*** of the agency. Hillary Clinton ignored this policy.
- Since 2009, NARA record management requirements stipulate regulations for emails using a system not operated by the Agency

  "Must ensure that federal records sent to or received on such systems are preserved in the appropriate agency and record keeping system."[ii]
  Hillary Clinton ignored this policy.

- NARA regulations require each agency to have a procedure to ensure that departing officials and employees do not remove federal records from agency custody.

The mere fact that all records were on a private server at a private residence clearly states that Hillary Clinton ignored this regulation. The separation statement called the DS – 109 specifically states

  "I have surrendered to responsible officials. All unclassified documents and papers related to the official business of the government acquired by me while in the employ of the department."

  She signed this and it was a lie. By doing so, she was committing a felony. The Emails were not supplied until 22 months later. They were only supplied then because Judicial Watch filed a lawsuit.

OIG Report Conclusions

Please note that the OIG report defines "non-departmental systems" as all non-agency PDAs and minicomputers.

FAM and FAH requirements for use of non-departmental systems are that they may only be turned on within departmental areas that are strictly non-secure such as a cafeteria. They are not allowed to be used in secure classified areas.

1. Hillary used PDAs in all her travels around the world including Russia and China in clear violation of these requirements.
2. Hillary was warned by the DOS with written and oral cautions not to use unprotected PDAs in her travels. She ignored these warnings.
3. The cyberthreat analysis division (CTAD) warned Hillary of cyber security risks associated with travel with the blackberry use in a foreign country but were ignored.

"The primary threat is traced to the Traveler's mobile device which is necessarily connected to the local cellular tower. The connection gives foreign entities the opportunity to intercept voice and email transmissions immediately after the traveler arrives overseas." [iii]

CONCLUSIONS

The 79-page OIG report clearly documents that Secretary Clinton felt herself above the law and above all State Department regulations. Further, she did not comply with any of the major security regulations to protect classified information. She did not turn in her Emails when she left the Department. Rather, it took a FOIA act and a lawsuit 22 months later to get some of the Emails (30,000 out of 61,000).

As a result, all of her communications in Russia, China, and every nation that she visited was using Plain Text Blackberry PDAs were compromised. They were open to anyone that had access to a computer. Further, she did not properly comply with FOIA requests. She did not supply all of the emails required on full disclosure. Rather she supplied 30,000 Emails as business relevant from her private server. It turns out that many of the Emails were classified and that this is a clear violation of the law and regulations. Specifically, 110 of those emails were top-secret, secret, and confidential; she clearly violated FRA, NARA, regulations which were felonious violations.

Finally, she violated common sense. Not anyone who does this should hold public office. She corresponded with everyone using plain text non-encrypted emails. This is worse than irresponsible. She cannot claim ignorance since she attended the mandatory Department of State security training meetings. Finally, it is important to note that on that server were all correspondence associated with her Clinton Fund that grew to $600 million with contributions from persons and nation states during her tenure. The FBI is currently doing a criminal review of the Clinton Fund.

JAMES COMEY

James Comey is an American lawyer that is currently the Director of the FBI. He made the decision to recommend to not indicting Hillary because she did not "Intend" to violate the law. Let us briefly examine some highlights of his professional background. Possibly, we can find some clues as to why this might happen given the clear evidence to the contrary.

Between 1996 and 2001, he was the Managing Assistant U.S. Attorney for the Eastern District of Virginia. In that capacity, he served as ***Deputy Special Counsel to the Senate Whitewater Committee***

This is significant and where Comey received his first exposure to the Clintons. Part 1 of this book documents this era. The Whitewater scandal started in Arkansas in 1977. I note that all participants to the Whitewater Scam went to jail except Bill and Hillary Clinton.

Mr. McDougal, the principal co-conspirator with the Clintons while serving a prison term in Arkansas was put into Solitary Confinement and suffered a heart attack - because he was not allowed to have access to his heart medicine.

The Senate Whitewater Committee was a special committee convened by the Senate at the beginning of the Clinton Administration. The U.S. Attorney out of Arkansas was "hot" on the heels of the Clintons when Bill Clinton was elected. One of Bill Clinton's first executive actions was to fire every U.S. Attorney in the country and reappoint each position. This had never been done before. Obviously, his pursuer, the U.S. Attorney from Arkansas was not re-appointed.

The Whitewater Committee was administered by the Senate Committee on Banking, Housing and Urban Affairs with Al D'Amato, Republican of NY, as chair.

> *"To conduct an investigation involving Whitewater Development Corporation, Madison Guaranty Savings and Loan Association, Capital Management Services, Inc., the Arkansas Development Finance Authority, and other related matters"*

On May 17, 1995, the committee ended its hearings. The committee's hearings ran for 300 hours over 60 sessions across 13 months, taking over 10,000 pages of testimony and 35,000 pages of depositions from almost 250 people; many of these marks were records for Senate committees. The committee issued an 800-page final majority report on June 18, 1996. Their conclusion was that there was not enough evidence to indict.

However, one of the critical pieces of evidence was missing. It was the billing records from the Rose Law Firm of Hillary Clinton. She was the principal advisor to Mr.

McDougal at Madison Guaranty Savings.

As noted, literally, everyone went to jail except the two Clintons. Hillary "lost" her billing records related to Madison Guaranty Savings and Loan Association – **the records showed up 2 years later in the upstairs library of the Presidential quarters.**

Pardon Gate- On January 20, 2001, James Comey again became involved with the Clintons. It related to Bill Clinton pardoning 20 felons on his last day in office. This was legal but many of these people gave the Clintons money for Hilary's Senate election race with donations to the Clinton Fund. Therefore, the timing of money then pardon left a "stink" in the press.

Comey oversaw the investigation of 20 people pardoned by President Clinton including Marc Rich after his wife gave the Clinton Foundation $450,000. Again, the pardons were within the Presidential prerogative. The donations and timings were suspicious. Knowing something happened and being able to prove it turns out to be a challenge.

Others gave "in kind" donations before their pardons. For instance, in return for Hillary support from the Latino community in New York, for her Senator race, Bill Clinton gave pardons to 16 murderers and bombers on his last day in office. Christopher Anderson relates that at Hillary's urging, Bill gave clemency to 16 Puerto Rican terrorists who took the lives of 16 Americans and wounded many others. Bill Clinton was then out of office and Hillary was running for the U.S. Senate.

Federal prosecutor and Democrat, Mary Jo White, was initially appointed to investigate the pardons. Republican James Comey replaced her. This was obviously a political play. However, I cannot find out what happened. The politics was played behind closed doors. Comey found no illegality on Clinton's part. However, these pardons were, according to retired President Carter, *"SHAMEFUL!"* I note that FDR believed that there are no coincidences in politics. I note that this is the **second time** that the Clintons were exonerated by James Comey.

IN 2002 – 2003 James Comey got his chance as a U.S. Attorney. This is an appointed not an elected position. Thus, it is a highly political position. Just prior to his stint in the AG's office, he served as the U.S. Attorney for the Southern District of New York. In December 2003, he appointed the Patrick Fitzgerald, a close friend, as Special Counsel to head the "CIA Leak" Grand Jury Investigation after John Ashcroft recused himself.

The *"Plame Affair"* refers to a leak from the CIA. On July 14, 2003, Robert Novak, a Washington Post reporter revealed the name of CIA employee Valerie Plame, wife of Joseph Wilson. Valerie was a covert agent for the CIA. On October 1, 2003, Richard Armitage told Colin Powell, Secretary of State and the FBI that he was the Robert Novak source. The issue was that Wilson, a former Ambassador, criticized the Bush Administration of *misrepresenting intelligence* regarding **"weapons of mass destruction"** prior to the 2003 invasion of Iraq. The nation went to war because of this misrepresentation. History shows that Wilson was right, there were no "Weapons of Mass Destruction" and the nation lost a trillion dollars and about 30,000 men wounded or killed in battle... However, the arms manufacturers made a lot of money, the bankers increased federal debt and they supported the Neocons in their fabricated war.

The issue here was misrepresentation to justify a war and exposure of all covert contacts of Valerie Plame for possible assassination. For James Comey, he was involved in squashing an exposure that helped the Democratic Party because it made the Republican President Bush look bad. Shortly thereafter, G.W. Bush gave him the job as second in command at the Justice Department.

During the 2003 – 2005 period, Comey served in the George W. Bush Administration (Jan 21, 2001 – Jan 21, 2009) as the Deputy Attorney General and ran day-to-day operations of the Department. He understands what goes on at Justice. He understands the law and the politics of protecting the incumbent.

During the period of August 2005 – 2013 he worked for some of the corporations that control America. Remember we have a fascist government that is best described as "corporatism". The Congress gives the corporations what they want and in turn, they give you funding for your reelection. Specifically, he worked as General Counsel at Lockheed and Bridgewater Associates as well as a short stint at Columbia Law School.

In late 2013, Barack Obama appointed him as FBI Director. Again, this means that he know that a portion of his job was to protect the incumbent in office – Obama.

Generally, it appears as if James Comey was always sensitive to his next politically appointed position. However, it appears as if he did a normal good job on his assignments. He has "let off" the Clintons **three times** now.

James Comey's Dual Standards

James Comey as Director of the FBI has had other cases where he acted and decided differently than the Hillary Clinton case. The question that we are examining is whether he uses a dual standard – one for the common man and another for the politician in office.

I will briefly discuss the Bryan H. Nashimura case and Hillary Clinton. In our nation, we have a Constitution and laws consistent with that Constitution. Our philosophy of government is that of Aristotle not that of Plato. We are a nation of laws that all have to follow not a nation run by an Emperor or a King who can override the law. The Aristotelian system of government requires that all people from the President on down to the lowest laborer comply with all the laws. We are now going to review two cases. In one case, Hillary Clinton was not indicted but in another case, a field engineer in Afghanistan was indicted. This clearly shows that Mr. Comey is "politically" sensitive and uses two standards for his recommendations.

The rulings both came from James Comey, FBI Director. In the Bryan H. Nashimura case, he was indicted for a felony for putting classified information on his personal devices such as a PDA or laptop. Hillary did far worse and exposed the US to grave danger in the potential loss of state secrets. Moreover, she had 10s of thousands of instances of doing this. Further, as Secretary of State, she traveled to Russia and China where everything said on her Blackberry PDA with high probability was captured and analyzed by foreign intelligence agencies. She was warned before she went to not use Blackberries in a foreign country but she did it anyway. This is a blatant and irresponsible thwarting of out federal laws on the control of records and the control of sensitive to top-secret information.

In order to see the clear differences in the two cases, I have provided a detailed comparison of the two's actions in spreadsheet that is labeled *Exhibit 1. Comparison of Clinton and Nashimura – Careless Handling of Classified Information*.

One can see from this comparison that the worst offender is Secretary of State, Hillary Clinton. FBI Director James Comey gave her a "pass" based upon her "intent" which is not measurable <u>nor is it relevant</u> since the law in question is a clear "stop sign" which says that <u>any</u> mishandling of classified information is a felony. It does not have to prove intent. The felony offense contains a punishment of

- Prison
- Fines
- *Permanent Removal of all security clearances*

If the last punishment were imposed, then Hillary Clinton would have to withdraw from the Presidential race.

WHO	WHAT
Bryan H. Nashimura	July , 2015
	Criminal charges for (1) having classified material on personal electronic devices that
	were "unatuthorized and unclassified" sytems - not authorized
	by the government to contain such Information.
	(2) No FBI evidence that he planned on distributing the information.was mentioned.
- Formal Charge	"Handled classified materials inappropriately" - Criminal Felony
	WHAT ACTUALLY HAPPENED
- Regional engineer	Afghanistan
- Deployed to Afghanistan	1. Removed and kept classified materials on
- Had access to classified	private devices - probably a laptop or thumb drive
briefings and digital records	drive for use at work station.
	2. FBI found the material in a search
SENTENCED and OUTCOME	
- Prison	Two years of Probation
- Fine	$7,600
- Media	Forfeiture of personal Media containing classified materials
- Security Clearance	PERMANENTLY SURRENDER ALL GOVERNMENT SECURITY CLEARANCES

Exhibit 1, Comparison of Clinton and Nashimura – Careless Handling of Classified Information

WHO	WHAT
Hillary Clinton	Jan 21, 2009 - Feb 1, 2013
- Formal Charge	NONE per FBI - James Comey - SHE HAD NO "INTENT" TO DO HARM
- Secretary of State	James Comey - " Although we did not find clear evidence that Secretary
- Had access to confidential, secret	Clinton or her colleagues intended to violate laws governing the handling
top secret and compartmentalized	of classified information, there is evidence that they were EXTREMELY
national secrets	CARELESS". - [Emphasis added]
- When traveling - used Blackberry	INTENT is not in the Law - only the mishandling creates a Felony offense.
- She had classified material on	
personal electronic devices that were	WHAT ACTUALLY HAPPENED
"unauthorized and unclassified systems	1. Removed and kept classified materials on
not authorized by the government to	private devices - PRIVATE SERVER, multiple ipads, multiple PDAs for she and her staff.
contain such information." - Felony	for use locally, non secure areas and global travel
per Bryan H. Nashimura	2. Clinton provided DOS and FBI 30,000 eMailis. Clinton took 31,000 "private"
	emails as determined by her private lawyers. FBI discovered 2,100 additional emails.
	These had additional classified information in them.
	3. Private server was hidden and not acknowledged until March 2015.
	4. Personal PDAs were Blackberry for she and her staff.
	- When off and battery still in, they can pass on local conversations
	- When transmitting in foreign countries - all conversations were in plain text and easily
	retrievabla by adversaraies. It is possible that all discussed state secrets were passed on.
	- Her home server had active attacks at least two times forcing it to be shut down.
	- Hackers, such as "Gustifer" had access to her server and exposed her
	correspondence with Blumenthal, her private advisory consultant.
	- Given that Gustifer had access, all foreign adversary intelligence agencies had access.
	The natonal State secrets were exposed posing Grave danger to the nation.
	5. Her formal exit from the State department required her to give back all government
	correspondence. She did not. It took a FOIA and a formal request from DOS in Dec 2014
	to get 30,000 emails. She kept 31,000 that SHE claimed were private.
	6. The number of emails on her server having classified data from the 30,000 provided
	- 110 emails and 52 chains
	- 8 Top Secret chains
	- 36 Secret chains
	- 8 Confidential Chains
	7. FBI- "We do assess that hostile actors gained access to the private commercial email
	accounts of people who Secretary Clinton was in regular contact from her personal
	account".
	8. FBI - Secretaary Clinton and her colleagues were "extremely careless in the
	handling of very sensitive, highly classifed information. "
	9. FBI - While outside of the U.S., including sending and receiving emials from
	sophisticated adversaries, she used personal emails.
	10. FBI NARROWED the investigation
	- Did Clinton Lie to Congress about her email practices? Not part of investigation
	- Did she conceal and illegally remove records? Not part of the investigation
	- No mention of the "Pay to Play" scheme of the Clinton Foundattion. Not part of the
	investigation.

Exhibit 1, Comparison of Clinton and Nashimura – Careless Handling of Classified Information

FBI Director James Comey - the Rule of Law – And Hillary Clinton

There are two ways to view Comey's action not to recommend indicting Hillary Clinton.

1. He saw ***the fix was in*** when Bill Clinton met with the AG, Lynch in her private jet and decided not to put his job on the line for a conflicted Obama Justice Department. The Fix was in and he would have to go along with it.
2. Try **to enforce the law**. To do this, he had to go along with Obama and Clinton but do it in a way that the American public would demand justice and force a prosecution. He used the technique of prosecuting the defendant before the public eye with the evidence against her and then finding a lame non-relevant reason to "let her off" by not recommending an indictment.

I do not know which one is the true motivation. He gives the appearance of going along with the "fix" but prosecutes with the evidence in a manner that justifies an indictment but does not ask for one. If the first one is the choice, the game is over. More obfuscation and cover up will occur.

However, one must remember that the following investigations are ongoing. He is deeply involved in the FBI criminal investigation of the Clinton Foundation / Fund. This will not come to a head until after the election in November.

- If Hillary Clinton wins, it will die.
- If Donald Trump wins, no one knows. He is also a political animal and may want political favors from the Democrats rather than Justice for the American people.

Investigation 1

A new Department of State investigation of the emails recently started.

Investigation 2

The FBI is still investigating the Clinton Foundation / Fund, which has associated emails on that Server. The FBI is in possession of the server and is forensically very sophisticated. To me this means that they have ALL the emails because they were recovered from the erased disc. This means that they have the emails even if they do not admit to having all of them. This is strong evidence considering that Hillary tried to remove and erase this evidence.

Investigation 3

There are ongoing investigations of the Emails that resided on the private server. Judicial Watch initiated the investigation and it has two sources. Judicial watch filed two FOIA actions with the U.S. State Department. The first was access to Hillary Clinton's Emails associated with Benghazi and the second was associated with the private server in her home. In both instances, the presiding Judge gave Judicial Watch the right to do a limited search through Hillary Clinton's Emails. It was not stated whether this included the 31,000, that she retained "private". It is highly likely that only the 30,000 were allowed to be searched. The 31,000 are the ones that contain the information.

SENIOR JUDGE ROYCE C. LAMBERTH, US DISTRICT COURT D.C.

It was because of the Judicial Watch Benghazi FOIA search that it was found that the State Department had none of Hillary's Emails. They were all on her private server in her home. The Judicial Watch FOIA request caused the State Department to demand the Emails back from Hillary. 30,000 of the 61,000 were returned in December 2014, which was 22 months after she left office. That was when they should have been returned.

Many knowledgeable people reacted negatively to the discovery of how Hillary and her staff had been handling Emails. Remember, the documented violations should have led to criminal charges involving violations of espionage statutes as well FRA, FISMA, NARA, FAM and FAH laws, regulations and State Department employee manuals.

Also, remember the server was in a private residence, unencrypted and with no firewalls. Some comments from experts in the field are worth reviewing.

Michael Hayden, a former director of NSA, the highest security agency in the US.

Government said [iv]

> *"If I was running a foreign intelligence service and I found out that Hillary Clinton had a private server, the next day I would have everything that was in the server on my desk. And, don't you believe that a number of foreign intelligence services didn't do exactly that?*

Joseph DiGenova, a former US attorney, told Judicial Watch [v]

> *This is a very serious matter. We have the person in line to be President of the United States who as Secretary of State set about at the beginning of her tenure, in 2009, to subvert the transparency of the United States government, to compromise national security, and then to lie about it repeatedly and laughing. This woman is not fit to be President of the United States."*

He speaks plainly. He said further that [vi]

> *"Let's put it this way. Last year, I said that the purpose of the private email server was to destroy history. Hillary Clinton wanted to hide, delete, evade, and prevent the disclosure of official government activity. The way she did it, and people who did it with her, who lied to federal courts about whether or not they had information, is a crime. There were crimes committed in front of Judge Sullivan in the form of false statements, and, ultimately, that*

will be part of the criminal case that the Justice Department has to review."

Finally, Mr. DiGenova names the conspirators. Rest assured, the list is broader than Hillary Clinton.[vii]

"Well, let me just say, the circle of figures at the center of the investigation includes Ms. Clinton, Mr. Patrick Pagliano, Huma Abedin, Patrick Kennedy, Cheryl Mills and several other people in the immediate circle. Those people all should have been privy to the fact that this was a private server and nothing else. They would have to know that the private server is not encrypted because they were using private, unencrypted devices to communicate with Ms. Clinton through the server. Every one of those people who has a high level of security clearance is a potential criminal target in that inner circle."

US Justice Royce Lamberth granted Judicial Watch, a government watchdog private organization, "limited discovery" on March 29, 2016 in response to a FOIA lawsuit. He did this because of the constant and steady Department of State stonewalling Judicial Watch was searching for records, Related to the drafting and use of the Benghazi talking points (Judicial Watch v. U.S. Department of State (No. 1:14-cv-01242)). Judge Lamberth said [viii]

"An understanding of the facts and circumstances surrounding Sec. Clinton's extraordinary and exclusive use of her Clinton mail.com account to conduct official government business, as well as other officials use of this account and their own personal email accounts to conduct official government business is required before the court can determine whether the search conducted here recently produce all responsive documents.

Plaintiff is certainly entitled to dispute the State Department's position that it has no obligation to produce these documents because it did not 'possess' or 'control' them at the time of the freedom of information act request was made."

Judge Emmett J Sullivan, U.S. District Court, DC.

In reference to the OIG report, Judge Sullivan said [ix]

"Well, that's good for the OIG and that's good for the FBI, but what about the public's right to know?"

There has been an ongoing effort by Judicial Watch to get records related to the hiring of Huma Abedin, Hillary's Deputy Chief of Staff. They had a lawsuit that was closed on March 9, 2014 but was reopened June 19, 2015 upon discovery of the private server or as the Judge put it, "revelations" about the Clintonemail.com system. (Judicial Watch v. U.S. Department of State is in (No.1:13-cv-01363)).

On February 23, 2016, US District Court (Washington D.C.) Emmett Sullivan granted Judicial Watch discovery into whether the State Department and Clinton **_deliberately thwarted the Freedom of Information Act for six years._** Judge Sullivan ruled in Judicial Watch's FOIA lawsuit that seeks records about the controversial employment status of Huma Abedin, former Deputy Chief of Staff for Hillary Clinton.

Judicial Watch filed a "narrowly tailored discovery" into Hillary Clinton's email. The discovery plan entails the testimony of witnesses and was filed on April 15, 2016

- Patrick Kennedy
- Bryan Pagliano, former State Department employee
- Cheryl Mills, aide to Clinton
- Huma Abedin, aide to Clinton

- Hillary Clinton if approved by Judge Sullivan Tom Fitton, the President of Judicial Watch, said [x]

"This remarkable decision will allow judicial watch to explore the shifting stories and misrepresentations made by the Obama State Department and its current and former employees. This Benghazi litigation first uncovered the Clinton email scandal, so it is good to have discovery in this lawsuit, which may help the American people find out why our efforts to get the Benghazi answers was thwarted by Clinton's email games."

Finally, we have a WikiLeaks Hillary Clinton Email that shows that her private needs exceed the government needs for classified information privacy. See the memo in Exhibit 2, WikiLeaks Clinton Email that says if there is no other way, remove the security, send it plain text, and send it non-secure. This is an attitude that will guaranty that this woman will get this nation into trouble if she ever holds a high-level position again.

```
From: H <hrod17@clintonemail.com>
Sent: Friday, June 17, 2011 8:21 AM
To: 'sullivanjj@ state.gov'

Subject: Re B5


If they can't, turn into nonpaper w no identifying heading and send nonsecure.

From: Sullivan, Jacob J [mailto:Sullivann@state.gov]
Sent: Friday, June 17, 2011 08:17 AM
To: H
Subject: Re: B5

They say they've had issues sending secure fax. They're working on it.
```

Exhibit 2, WikiLeaks Clinton Email

FBI Director James Comey – The Fix Is In v. American People

One cannot but wonder why James Comey during his announcement about the conclusions from the FBI server investigation made the case for indictment and then did not recommend indictment. I must postulate what was going on. Only Comey knows and he is not talking. Let us look as the alternatives.

Alternative 1 – The Fix Is In

In this instance, Comey knew that if he recommended indictment, the Justice Department would still let Hillary go free. In addition, he knew that he would lose his job before Jan 20, 2017.

It turns out that there are two justice department managers between himself and the Attorney General, Loretta Lynch. He knew that Lynch probably recused herself because of her meeting with Bill Clinton - which might have been prearranged to allow her to recuse herself.

Remembering that his role as FBI Director is to be a policeman. His job is to do data gathering on the potential crime not to use prosecutorial judgment. Lynch put him into a position to recommend an action, which is her job. Specifically, her job is to conclude from the evidence whether the party under investigation should be prosecuted.

What to do? He must let her off to preserve his job. However, he could do it in a way to lay out the case against Hillary and then recommend not prosecuting. This is what he did. As a result, the American people saw the case, saw some of the evidence, were in disbelief, and disappointed that the FBI sullied its reputation for this political purpose.

There is risk here but not as much as recommending indictment and prosecution.

Alternative 2 – Let the American People Decide

Let us consider this alternative and pose a way that it could come about.

Comey is not a stupid. Although, he may have been directed to recommend freedom with his Hillary announcement, he may have figured out a way for her to be exposed in another way. The FBI has no authority to make decisions whether or not to prosecute crimes; they only investigate and the Justice Department decides whether to prosecute or not.

This is speculation but is seems reasonable. Suppose he decided to do something out of the ordinary — lay out and disclose most of his evidence during his Press Conference. He knew what he was doing and he knew that it would create a "firestorm" of controversy. If he had gone internal and sent everything he had to AG Lynch, it might have all been buried or, at least, not disclosed until long after the election. Instead, he threw it all out for the public to know. Let's examine what was said during the July 5, 2016 Comey Announcement [xi]

Quote 1

"I did not email any classified material to anyone on my email. There is no classified material...." Hillary Clinton, March 10, 2015

"Seven email chains concern matters that were classified at the top- secret/special access program level when they were sent and received. These chains involve Secretary Clinton both sending emails about those matters and receiving emails." James Comey, July 5, 2060

Quote 2

"Nothing I said was more classified work that received was marked classified", March 7, 2016

"Even if information is not marked classified in an email, participants who know, or should know, that the subject matter is classified are still obligated to protect it." James Comey, July 5, 2015

Quote 3

**"I think classified information seriously."
Hillary Clinton, February 1, 2016**

"... There is evidence they were extremely careless in their handling of very sensitive, highly classified information." James Comey, July 5, 2016[xii]

James Comey knew that the material released would cause Congress to *call for an investigation*. Further, he knew Congress would react. Moreover, they did

"While we need more information about how the bureau came to this recommendation, the American people will reject this troubling pattern of dishonesty and poor judgment," House Speaker Paul Ryan said in a formal statement

The result of that investigation will be that he will answer Congress' Questions. If Hillary is convicted of Criminal actions, the burden will fall upon the Congress not the Executive Branch. He made himself available almost instantly (tomorrow at 10 AM) knowing that they will want to dig even deeper, hear about more evidence and have an open-ended Q&A for the entire day if they want to. If he wanted to, he could have stalled this for a month or so.

It is reasonable to think Comey knew that in this manner, the FBI's entire case would get a full public airing; also, since there is not a prosecution pending, he can be candid and open about anything and everything.

He knew that if it went to the Justice Department, the case would die a "slow death" there. *Nothing will be kept secret now*; we will learn about things (such as Hillary having 12 private servers) that no one even suspected existed. James Comey can try this case before the public, just as he started to do laying out the key evidence before *"dropping the case"* at his public announcement. Everyone thought he was heading toward a recommendation of prosecution and then he surprised everyone.

The Public and Media will now get to know EVERYTHING that would or could have been presented in court if there was a prosecution. In fact, even more than what could be presented in court because there will be no rules of evidence holding him back. This hearing could prove to be extremely eye opening.

This approach implies that Comey might have outsmarted Lynch and Obama when they told him to *"kill this case"*. A Grand Jury might have taken 6 months or longer to accomplish this type of detailed inquiry, if run properly. In addition, Grand Juries are secret, except for leaks. Now ***nothing will be secret***.

If this scenario plays out, Comey might prove that he is no one's "lackey"; however, he will just "play it straight"

- Answer all of the questions and not have to volunteer anything.
- Obama and Lynch cannot tell him to lie to Congress.

He might have looked foolish laying out this case when not recommending prosecution but he might be wiser beyond our thinking because now he will just be responding to questions "under oath".

This is my take on a possible near-future scenario. This could come out to be the only way to take down a liar and dishonest government official who is being "protected".

People like this need the full light of exposure. Darkness and secrecy is the only way they can function. It the scenario evolves this way, it could prove to be worse than anything Hillary and Bill ever imagined. It is also possible for the Congressional inquiry to evolve into the Clinton Foundation that was presumably also on this server.

I hope that if justice can overtake our corrupt government, this will happen.

HILLARY'S RECORD OF BURYING EMAILS

Before we investigate the Clinton Foundation, let us do a quick review of other instances where the Clintons have used delay and deletion of emails /evidence to remain free.

1.   Project X_1999

As first lady, Hillary was embroiled in another scheme to bury sensitive White House emails, known internally as "Project X."

In 1999, as investigators looked into Whitewater, Travelgate, Filegate and other scandals involving the then-first lady, it was discovered that more **than _1 million subpoenaed emails were mysteriously "lost" due to a "glitch" in a West Wing computer server._**

The massive hole in White House archives covered a critical two-year period (1996 to 1998) when Republicans and special prosecutor Ken Starr were subpoenaing White House emails. This dwarfs the missing minutes on the "Nixon tapes"

Despite separate congressional investigations and a federal lawsuit over Project X, high-level emails dealing with several scandals were **never** turned over. In addition, the full scope of Bill and Hillary Clinton's culpability in the parade of scandals was never known.

2.   Secret Server

Thanks to another server-related problem, Clinton so far has gotten away with withholding more than 30,000 emails from congressional committees investigating the Benghazi terrorism cover-up, the hiring of Abedin and the Clinton Foundation foreign-influence peddling.

> *"This Clinton email scandal is nothing new,"* Judicial Watch president Tom Fitton, said, *"There were previous efforts to hide emails in the Clinton White House."*

Fitton's Judicial Watch Washington watchdog group filed a lawsuit to recover the missing White House emails back then, just as it has against the State Department now. It has had better luck in this case. He had consistently lost against the Clintons. However, recently with Judges Sullivan and Lamberth, he appears to have made headway.

The parallels do not end there.

During the Project X Email scandal, career White House staffers and contractors found that someone close to the first lady had turned off the White House's automated email archiving system. They fingered White House *"special assistant"* Laura Crabtree Callahan, who was overseeing the computer contractors despite obtaining computer science degrees from diploma mills.

The State Department staffer who set up Clinton's unsecured server in the basement of Clinton's home in Chappaqua also lacked computer experience and qualifications. That IT staffer, Bryan Pagliano, appears to be playing a similar role in this email caper as Callahan did in the White House — that of a lackey used to help thwart public requests to see information about the government-related businesses of the Clintons.

Despite having no computer security experience or even security clearance, Pagliano catapulted from a Clinton **_campaign worker_** to the secretary's own "special adviser" dealing with the department's classified email system.

On top of his $133,000-a-year State Department salary, Clinton personally paid Pagliano thousands of dollars between 2009 and 2013 to set up and run a private home-brew server for her, separate from the government system she was supposed to use. This is where she received and stored 30 thousand government emails of which 110 were classified. His work for the secretary was a rogue operation, because the department's inspector general found that his boss, the deputy chief information officer, was *"unaware of his technical support of the secretary's email system."*

Like Callahan before him, Pagliano had unusual access to Clinton. The one qualification they shared was apparently the one that mattered most: "loyalty to the queen".

Both appear to have been sworn to secrecy about the email diversions. Pagliano took the Fifth when called to testify before Congress

When career staffers at State raised concerns that Clinton's email records were not being properly captured and preserved, they were told to *"shut up"*, according to the OIG report, instructed, *"**never to speak of the secretary's personal email system again**."*

Likewise, career staffers and contractors at the White House were ordered to keep those earlier "not archived" emails secret. In fact, they testified that Callahan personally *"threatened them with jail time if they disclosed the gap to prosecutors or lawmakers."*

Cheryl Mills now finds herself in the middle of an investigation into the whereabouts of thousands of emails germane to investigations involving Hillary Clinton that also have conveniently turned up missing. It was Mills who helped her old boss remove some 32,000 emails from the server Pagliano set up, claiming they were irrelevant to investigations. Yet no one in the State Department ever saw those Emails.

3. Missing Whitewater Documents [xiii]

The record of Hillary's billings from the Rose Law Firm related to the Whitewater Land fraud disappeared. The Senate Whitewater committee wanted them to determine her involvement. The records turned up 2 years later after the investigation was finished in the White House private residence library. Her physical fingerprints were on them.

She is the only First Lady that has ever been fingerprinted. These files were last seen in Vince Foster's office and were reportedly removed by Hillary's staff after the Foster "suicide" was reported and the Park Police sealed the office (2 days later). The Secret Service reported that Cheryl Mills removed some files but they did not see which ones.

4. Missing Travelgate Documents

The Day before the Whitewater investigation, a missing letter showed up according the New York Times that showed that Hillary was deeply involved in the firing of the Whitehouse travel agency people. Vince Foster at her direction fired them.

5. Hillary and Watergate

According to Democrat Jerry Zeifman, Hillary **"engaged in unethical practices in violation of House rules."** Specifically, Zeifman accused Hillary Rodham of writing a fraudulent legal brief and grabbing public documents. Zeifman fired her for lying and later claimed that he wished he had reported her to the bar.

CONCLUSION

Over a period of 39 years, there have been 5 instances of missing files. Each time, the missing files were evidence in criminal investigations. Each time, the lack of the files at the critical time led to Hillary Clinton being not indicted. The only marginal case was Watergate, but as her manager said, he should have reported her to the bar for disbarment.

HILLARY'S PRESIDENTIAL PROBLEM: BILL CLINTON AND UNITED ARAB REPUBLIC XIV

Hillary and Bill are a tag team of corruption. Bill Clinton has had a five-year business relationship with Dubai's ruler, Sheikh Mohammed bin-Rashid al-Maktoum. The UAE is a group of states that include Dubai. The history goes like this.

- Bill Clinton asked bin-Rashid to join him as a business partner through his Dubai Investment Group. At the time, he was the Crown Prince.
- The two did their private financial deals with Yucaipa Partners, a California private equity fund owned by billionaire Rob Burkle.
  - They tried to create an offshore wealth fund for Yucaipa.
  - Clinton ended the relationship 5 years later according to the Daily Beast
    - *He took $15 million in guaranteed payments*
    - *He took another $20 million in walk away money*
- Today, Bill Clinton visits Dubai often.
  - Human rights groups claim the labor practices are bad and that the UAE exploit 250,000 foreign laborers.
  - World Employment and Social Outlook Report says that the Persian Gulf governments use *"forced labor, modern slavery, human trafficking and the worst forms of child labor."*

- o 4 billionaire Saudis, Dubai Foundation and Friends of Saudi Arabia – contributed $30 million to the Clinton Foundation.
- o Bill Clinton took $5.6 million from a Dubai company, GEMS education, to be an "***honorary chairman***" with no duties.
- As Secretary of State, Hillary approved
  - o Speaking engagements for Bill that earned $1.1 million in fees.
  - o In 2012, she hosted a State Department conference attended by executives from 90 American companies.
  - o In December 2011, Hillary led a U.S. delegation to the UAE and met bin-Rashid at his Zabeel palace and Sheikh Abdullah bin Zayed. The Zayed family gave $1 to $5 million to the Clinton Foundation.
  - o The purchase by Russia UrAsia, which owned 20% of the US production in Uranium.
- As Secretary of State, Hillary she
  - o Showed disregard for protecting national classified information
  - o Put classified information on unprotected PDA, iPads, laptops and servers
  - o Did not return state business information when she left office.
  - o Talked and messaged in foreign countries with plain text unprotected Blackberries.
  - o Put state classified information on unsecure devices with
    - ▪ No firewall
    - ▪ No encrypted data path
    - ▪ No pass word verification
    - ▪ No encrypted data bases
    - ▪ Possibly no backup – never mentioned

CONCLUSIONS

We have found that the law is clear and simple with respect to classified material. "Intent" is not mentioned. If you do not handle classified material with care and keep it on government safe equipment, you have violated the law, which is a felony. The mere act of being careless is the felony. Intent is not even looked upon as relevant.

Clearly, Hillary violated the law and committed multiple felonies. She put classified material on unsafe insecure servers, PDAs, laptops and iPads. Further, she outfitted her staff with the same equipment and they communicated with each other as if they were just friends – not representatives of the U.S. Government with state secrets to protect.

Clearly, against the oral and written advice of DOS security people, she used PDAs in foreign travel that exposed her conversations and others related to state secrets open for disclosure. The FBI said that those that she communicated with had penetrations. To me this means that their systems were passively attacked and information relayed to them by her was stolen.

Her actions were far worse than the engineer, Bryan Nashimura, who was found guilty and had his security clearances removed. She had at least two active attacks on her server that she admits happened.

Further, when she left public office, she did not return government emails per the law and the State Department regulations. This is another felony. Upon action of a FOIA and a lawsuit, the state department retrieved 30,000 of the 61,000 emails 22 months after she left office. The choice of whether the email message was private or not was made by her private attorneys not the DOS attorneys. In the 30,000 Emails returned, 110 emails contained top secret, secret and confidential material that was resident on her PRIVATE server. Never in the history of the U.S. has anyone done this before. Her claim that others did this is another Hillary "Lie".

PART 2

THE CLINTON FUND

THE CLINTON FUND

The Clinton Fund is not "organized crime" as reported in many places on the internet. However, it is a sophisticated method of tax avoidance that enables

- The "disappearance" of critical records when the owners want that to happen.
- Hiding of donor names in a Canadian Charity
- Hiding any purpose of the donation and correspondence that could be used in any extortion probe.
- Difficulty in matching source of funds with destination of funds.

Nonetheless, the Clinton Fund it is currently under a criminal investigation by the FBI. The FBI does not say what why it is being investigated.

With that said, let us examine how the fund is set up and some of the fund's history. Currently, it has $2 billion in funds and 2,000 employees according to WikiLeaks.

Charitable foundation watchdogs have made a number of observations on the Clinton fund. They are illuminating. Here are some comments

- Charity Navigator –They put the Clinton Fund on its watch list and notified potential donors about investing in "Problematic charities".
- Sunlight Foundation – Bill Allison, senior fellow, *"It seems like the Clinton Foundation operates as a slush fund for the Clintons."*

In July 2013, Eric Braverman, a friend of Chelsea Clinton, became the CEO of the Clinton Foundation. He started at $275,000 and went to $395,000 a year later as reported by Politico.

How It Works

1. Remember, the goal is to hide income from taxes, maintain secrecy and provide virtually unlimited funds for the Clintons in travel and their special projects. Here is how it works:

   1. Create the Clinton Fund, which is a Foundation. It is a charitable 501 (C3) that is tax-free.

2. Create or find a foreign "charity" In this case, it is in Canada. This Canadian Charity cooperates in conjunction with the Clinton Foundation. This is convenient because the Clintons claim that the cooperating Canadian charity by law prohibits the identification of individual donors. It is not true. The Canadian government does not require that.

3. Get foreign individuals and governments to donate to the Canadian charity. This is how they stay anonymous.

4. What do these people get in return? No one knows. <u>That is why the Clinton fund and the Canadian Charity need secrecy.</u> It is why the emails from the server are so important.

5. I note this Email removal was an illegal act since at that point (22 months after leaving office) they were Department of State assets not private assets. She did not remove them prior to leaving which was her right. Further, the Department of State attorneys should have done that selection not her private attorneys (probably Cheryl Mills).

6. Get your foreign donors to give to the Canadian Charity that in turn bundles the gifts and gives them to the Clinton Foundation. This is the way they remove the source of funds.

7. The Clinton Foundation then "spends" some of this money for legitimate good works programs. Experts believe this is about 10%.

The balance goes to the Clintons to pay salaries of up to 2,000 people, some of whom are in a holding pattern for the Clinton's to tap them for government service when, in their belief, Hillary becomes president This is all tax free, which means you and I are subsidizing it. It was announced that the Clinton Presidential campaign funds have also been folded into this Clinton Fund.

8. Tax Fillings - The Clinton Fund, with access to the world's best accountants, fails to report much of these transactions on their tax filings. They then discover these "clerical errors" and begin the process of re-filing 5 years of tax returns.

9. Intended net result — foreign money, much of it from national treasuries and rich oligarchs goes into the Clinton's pockets tax free and is untraceable back to the original donor. This appears to me to be the textbook definition of money laundering. Let us examine why I say.

Most anti-money laundering laws in the financial system are concerned with _source_ of funds and _destination_ of funds. The destination of funds is usually terrorism financing. In this instance, governments and individuals are the source of funds and the destination of the funds is stated as charity – The Clinton Foundation - when it is in fact the Clintons. This is Fraud. You promise A – charity but deliver B – Clinton Fund – a charitable trust controlled by the Clintons and used as a private slush fund. If you wanted the Clintons to use it as a slush fund, then it should be taxable to them.

Some countries define money laundering as obfuscating sources of money, either intentionally or by merely using financial systems or services that do not identify or track sources or destinations. This is clearly happening here. Further, other countries define money laundering to include money from activity A that _would have been_ a crime in that country, even if it were legal where the actual conduct occurred. In this instance, the foreign source of money sent to a Charitable Foundation of a sitting Secretary of State would be illegal if the Secretary of State actions helped the foreign national in any way. This is bribery and extortion.

FRANK GIUSTRA

Frank Giustra (59) lives in Vancouver. As a child, he lived in Italy and Argentina. He graduated from high school in British Columbia where he majored in music and switched to business at Douglas College. His father was a Sudbury, CA nickel miner who introduced him to his broker.

He began his investment industry career in 1978 with Merrill Lynch as an assistant trader and eventually a stockbroker. He left the company in the early 80s to found a resource-financing group for Yorktown Securities where he worked. He was appointed chairman and CEO. From 2001-2007, Giustra was chair of Endeavour Financial, a merchant banking firm which financed mining companies. He is now the CEO of the Fiore Group of companies.

Just as the mining sector collapsed, Mr. Giustra, a lifelong film buff, founded the Lion's Gate Entertainment Corporation in 1997. He sold the studio in 2003 and returned to mining.

PHILANTHROPY AND CLINTON

In 1997, Giustra established the Radcliffe Foundation and was its president. The Vancouver-based foundation supports local and international disaster relief, economic development and homelessness charities.

In June 2007, Giustra launched the **Clinton Giustra Enterprise Partnership** (CGEP) with U.S. President Bill Clinton. It is a partnership between the William J. Clinton Foundation, the private sector foundation and **governments**, local communities, and other NGOs to increase the scope and scale where poverty is widespread. Note that it is set up to receive donations from governments.

CGSGI aims to alleviate poverty in the developing world in partnership with the global mining community. He and Carlos Slim, Mexican billionaire, have pledged a minimum $100 million each toward the effort. In addition, **Giustra pledged one-half of whatever he makes the rest of his life to CGEP.**

On June 17, 2010, Giustra teamed up with Carlos Slim and President Clinton to create a $20 million fund that will finance small businesses in earthquake-ravaged Haiti.

WHY DID THE CLINTONS TEAM WITH GIUSTRA?

The Clintons seldom do things without a purpose. Given that they have a strong desire for secrecy, it seems reasonable that this foreign-to-domestic laundering scheme satisfies a number of key Clinton objectives. Let us examine a few.

- It gave Secretary of State Hillary Clinton <u>plausible deniability</u> about the millions in foreign cash that were being funneled into her family's non-profit coffers.
  - She <u>wasn't on the board of CGEPartnership</u>, and
  - She was not named to the board of the Clinton Foundation until 2013 – after her tenure as Secretary of State.
  - It gave Hillary's allies the <u>ability to claim that wealthy foreign individuals were not sending cash to the Clinton Foundation</u> because they were sending it to the CGEPartnership.
  - Bill Clinton never served on board of CGEP while Hillary was Secretary of State
  - <u>Bill Clinton placed Bruce Lindsey on the CGEPartnership board</u>. Lindsey was a long time Bill Clinton advisor who serves as the Chairman of the Board of the Clinton Foundation. He was the <u>CEO of the Clinton Foundation for over 10 years.</u>
  - The Scheme setup has everything they need
    - Massive cash flow to CGEPartnership
    - Refusal to disclose donors at CGEPartnership. There is NO Canadian law that says that donors could not be disclosed. This is false but adds to their secrecy.
    - The Secret and now disappeared emails (31,000) that probably contained the correspondence with the Sheiks and others

documenting any conflicts of interest if there are any. I note the Hillary only said that the emails were removed. She never said that they were destroyed.

- Blatantly falsified tax returns and resubmission upon resubmission.
- Bogus Excuses such as the Canadian law does not allow disclosure. In fact, it does and these donors have been disclosed in Canada but not the U.S...

URANIUM - THE DEAL THAT BROUGHT MASSIVE "DONATIONS" TO THE CGEP AND CLINTON FUND

A story in the NY Times in Jan 2008 describes what happened between the Clinton Fund and Frank Giustra to clinch the Uranium mining sale to the Russians. The FBI should closely investigate this one deal.

Former President Bill Clinton with Sir Tom Hunter (on the left) and Frank Giustra (on the right), major donors to Mr. Clinton's charitable Clinton Fund are shown in the NY Times news photo.

Late on Sept. 6, 2005, a private plane carrying the Canadian mining financier Frank Giustra landed in Almaty, a city in southeast Kazakhstan. This nation had highly coveted deposits of uranium that could fuel nuclear reactors around the world. Mr. Giustra was in pursuit of an exclusive deal to tap them.

Mr. Giustra was a newcomer to uranium mining in Kazakhstan, a former Soviet republic but not to mining operations. He had many connections. Accompanying Mr. Giustra on his luxuriously appointed MD-87 jet that day was a former president of the United States, Bill Clinton.

This was the first stop of a three-country "philanthropic" tour. The two men were taken to a midnight banquet with Kazakhstan's president, Nursultan A. Nazarbayev.

The NY Times says this is what happened –

- Mr. Nazarbayev <u>walked away from the table with a propaganda coup</u>, after Mr. Clinton expressed enthusiastic

support for the Kazakh leader's bid to head an international organization that monitors elections and supports democracy.
- It is a fact that Mr. Nazarbayev is a dictator with a horrible human rights record. Democracy means that he always wins the elections with over 95% majority.
- Bill Clinton's public declaration undercut both American foreign policy and sharp criticism of Kazakhstan's poor human rights record by others including Hillary Rodham Clinton.
- Within two days after leaving, Mr. Giustra came up a winner when his company signed preliminary agreements giving it the right to buy into three uranium projects controlled by Kazakhstan's state-owned uranium agency, Kazatomprom. This is the only way get access to the Kazakhstan uranium – the largest deposits in the world.

The monster deal stunned the mining industry, turning an unknown shell company into one of the world's largest uranium producers in a transaction ultimately worth tens of millions of dollars to Mr. Giustra, analysts said.

THEN CAME THE REWARD

Within a few months after the Kazakh pact was finalized, Mr. Clinton's charitable foundation received

- A $31.3 million donation from Mr. Giustra that had remained a secret until he acknowledged it in December 2007.
- Entrance to Bill Clinton's inner circle - That gift, combined with Mr. Giustra's public pledge to give the William J. Clinton Foundation an additional $100 million secured Mr.Giustra a place in Mr. Clinton's inner circle.
  - o Mr. Giustra was invited to accompany the former president to Almaty just as the financier was trying to seal a deal he had been negotiating for months.
  - o Both men said Mr. Giustra traveled with Mr. Clinton to Kazakhstan, India and China to see first-hand the philanthropic work done by Bill Clinton's Foundation.

- ○ Mr. Giustra said he was there as an "observer only" and there was "no discussion" of the deal with Mr. Nazarbayev or Mr. Clinton.
- ○ Moukhtar Dzhakishev, president of Kazatomprom (Kazakhstan nationalized oil company), said in an interview that Mr. Giustra
  - Did discuss it, directly with the Kazakh president, and
  - His friendship with Mr. Clinton *"of course made an impression."*
  - After hearing Mr. Dzhakishev's statements, Mr. Giustra said he *"May have well mentioned my general interest in the Kazakhstan mining business to him, but I did not discuss the ongoing efforts."*

Bill Clinton has vowed to continue raising money for his foundation if Mrs. Clinton is elected president, maintaining his connections with a wide network of philanthropic partners.

Mr. Giustra said that while his friendship with the former president *"may have elevated my profile in the news media, it has not directly affected any of my business transactions."*

Neil MacDonald, the chief executive of a Canadian merchant bank that specializes in mining deals, said Mr. Giustra's financial success was partly due to a "fantastic network" crowned by Mr. Clinton. Mr. MacDonald said. *"I'm sure it's very much a two-way."*

Mr. Giustra's timing on the acquisition was impeccable. He bought the company for $32 per share in 2005. Uranium then tripled in price and he sold it at $113 per share in April 2007 for $3.1 billion.

The two were introduced in June 2005 at a fund-raiser for tsunami victims at Mr. Giustra's Vancouver home and hit it off right away. They share a love of history, geopolitics and music — Mr. Giustra plays the trumpet to Mr. Clinton's saxophone. Soon the dapper Canadian was a regular at Mr. Clinton's side, as they flew around the world aboard Mr. Giustra's plane.

ENERGY

Let us back up for a moment, in 2003 and 2004, the world population was growing and the demand for energy was growing. Obama's war on coal left oil, gas and nuclear. By far the cleanest is nuclear. Uranium, the raw material for reactor fuel, was about to become a hot commodity. In late 2004, Mr. Giustra began talking to investors, and put together a company that would eventually be called - *UrAsia Energy*

Things get complex from here on. The meetings get to be confusing. Thus, I put together a Spreadsheet that lists all the dates and events up to Russia takeover of the US largest mining operation of uranium in this nation. Russia now owns 20% of US production. **Exhibit 3, Dates and Events Leading Up to Russia Takeover of 20% of US Uranium Production.** You can use it to follow what happens until Dec 2013 when the final transaction takes place. Hillary Clinton as Secretary of State approved this transaction.

DATE	EVENT
2004	**Giustra forms UrAsia**
Jul-05	**SXR Uranium Resources formed from Merger**
	- Southern Cross Resources
	- Aflease Gold
Jul-05	**Bill Clinton and Giustra meet for 1ˢᵗ time**
Aug-05	**UrAsia / Giustra sends his mining engineer to Kazakhstan**
6-Sep-05	**Giustra and Bill Clinton fly to Kazakhstan**
	Meet President Nursultan Nazarbayev
	1. Bill Clinton suggests that Nazarbayev
	become Chairman of European "Organization for
	Security and Cooperation" a Human Rights Org
	This is just the opposite Nazarbayev - a dictator
	Nazarbayev wanted the position to mine

	2. Bill Clinton introduces Giustra as Uranium minor
	wanting to develop Uranium mining in Kazakhstan
	3. Nazarbayev says proceed with mining
8-Sep-05	UrAsia / Giustra receive $450 million contract from Kazakhstan
1-Nov-05	Clinton Foundation receives $31.3 million from Giustra
	Additional $100 million pledged by Giustra
Nov-05	UrAsia Canadian IPO raises $450 million
Dec-05	1. Nazarbayev becomes Chair of European Human Rights
	organization - Organization for Security and Cooperation
	2. Nazarbayev wins election with "ballot stuffing"
	3. Kazakhstan / UrAsia deal completed
Sep-06	Giustra throws 60th birthday party for Bill Clinton
	a. $21 million raised for Clinton Fund
	b. Total Raised to date - $100 million pledge + 31.3 + 21 =
	$152.3 million
Feb-07	SXR Uranium Resources acquires controlling interest in UrAsia
	$3.1 billion paid
2009	ARMZ (Russian government) acquires 16.6% interest in
	SXR Uranium One
	a. Uranium One owns largest U.S. uranium mine
	Uranium One Deal Approved by Hillary Clinton Secretary of State
Dec-13	ARMZ (Russian government) acquires 100% of SXR Uranium One

	a. Rosatrom (Russia State Energy) owns 100% of ARMZ
	b. Rosatrom dissolves ARMZ
	c. Rosatrom owns 100 % of old UrAsia uranium assets and mining in Kazakhstan and the USA (20% of all uranium)

Exhibit 3, Dates and Events Leading Up to Russia Takeover of 20% of US Uranium Production

Kazakhstan, which has about one-fifth of the world's uranium reserves, was the place to be in 2005. However, with plenty of suitors, Kazatomprom could be meticulous about its partners. A second-tier player like UrAsia needed all the help it could get.

The Cameco Corporation, the world's largest uranium producer, was already a partner of Kazatomprom. However, when Cameco expressed interest in the properties Mr. Giustra was already eying, the government's response was lukewarm. *"The signals we were getting was - you've got your hands full,"* said Gerald W. Grandey, Cameco president.

For Cameco, the world's largest uranium producer took five years to *"build the right connections"* in Kazakhstan, Mr. Grandey said. UrAsia did not have that luxury.

In August 2005, records show, the company sent an engineering consultant to Kazakhstan to assess the uranium properties. Less than four weeks later, Mr. Giustra arrived with Mr. Clinton. Note they met in July 2005, a month later, they sent in the engineer; then 2 months later they go to Kazakhstan.

Mr. Dzhakishev, the Kazatomprom chief, said an aide to Mr. Nazarbayev informed him that Mr. Giustra talked with Mr. Nazarbayev about the deal during the visit. *"And when our president asked Giustra, 'What do you do?'* he said, *'I'm trying to do business with Kazatomprom,'"* Mr. Dzhakishev said. He added that Mr. Nazarbayev replied, *"Very good, go to it."*

Mr. Clinton's Kazakhstan visit publicly stated reason for the visit was to announce a Clinton Foundation agreement that enabled the government to buy discounted AIDS drugs. However, during a news conference, Mr. Clinton wandered into delicate territory by commending Mr. Nazarbayev for *"opening up the social and political life of your country"* – which he had not done.

In a statement Kazakhstan would highlight in news releases, Mr. Clinton declared that he hoped it would achieve a top objective: leading the *"Organization for Security and Cooperation in Europe"* – a human rights organization -, which would confer legitimacy on Mr. Nazarbayev's government. *"I think it's time for that to happen, it's an important step, and I'm glad you're willing to undertake it,"* Mr. Clinton said. Kazakhstan wanted this prize. He had a deservedly bad human rights reputation and this would help him appear as a world leader that was balanced.

Mr. Clinton's praise was odd, given that the United States did not support Mr. Nazarbayev's bid and Hillary Clinton had voiced skepticism because of serious corruption, canceled elections and government control of the news media. He received the position by the end of the year. In a written statement to <u>The Times</u>, Mr. Clinton's spokesman said the former president saw *"no contradiction"* between his statements in Kazakhstan and the position of Mrs. Clinton, who said through a spokeswoman, *"Senator Clinton's position on Kazakhstan remains unchanged."* The positions were in fact completely opposite of one another.

Robert Herman worked for the State Department in the Clinton administration and is now at Freedom House, a human rights group. He said the former president's statement amounted to an endorsement of Kazakhstan's readiness to lead the group, a position he called "patently absurd."

Mr. Clinton with Nursultan A. Nazarbayev, president of Kazakhstan, in September 2005. CreditProsites- Kazakhembus. Homstead.com

In December 2005, Mr. Nazarbayev won another election, with an "atmosphere of intimidation" and "ballot-box stuffing. This was reported by the security organization itself.

Within 48 hours of Mr. Clinton's departure from Almaty on Sept. 7, Mr. Giustra got his deal. UrAsia signed two memorandums of understanding that paved the way for the company to become partners with Kazatomprom in three mines.

The cost to UrAsia was more than $450 million, money the company did not have in hand and had only weeks to come up with. The transaction was finalized in November, after UrAsia raised the money through the largest initial public offering in the history of Canada's Venture Exchange.

Longtime market watchers were confounded. Kazatomprom's choice of UrAsia was a ***"mystery,"*** said Gene Clark, the chief executive of Trade Tech, a uranium industry newsletter.

> ***"UrAsia was able to jump-start the whole process somehow,"*** Mr. Clark said. The company became a ***"major uranium producer when it didn't even exist before."***

One year later, in September 2006, Mr. Giustra co-produced a gala 60th birthday for Mr. Clinton that featured stars like Jon Bon Jovi and raised about $21 million for the Clinton Foundation. Thus, the donations so far were $100 + $31.3 + $21 million = $152.3 million.

6 Months later, in February 2007, a company called Uranium One agreed to pay $3.1 billion to acquire UrAsia. Mr. Giustra, a director and major shareholder in UrAsia, would be paid $7.05 per share for a company that just two years earlier was trading at 10 cents per share.

That same month, Mr. Dzhakishev, the Kazatomprom chief, said he traveled to Chappaqua, N.Y., to meet with Mr. Clinton at his home. Mr. Dzhakishev said Mr. Giustra arranged the three-hour meeting. Mr. Dzhakishev said he wanted to discuss Kazakhstan's intention — not publicly known at the time — **to buy a 10 percent stake in Westinghouse, a United States supplier of nuclear technology. They make the Atomic plants.**

Mr. Dzhakishev said he was worried the proposed Westinghouse investment could face similar objections to the 5 Port deal that was killed by our Congress. Mr. Clinton told him that he would not lobby for him, but Mr. Dzhakishev came away pleased by the chance to promote his nation's proposal to a former president.

Mr. Clinton "said this was very important for America," said Mr. Dzhakishev, who added that **Mr. Giustra was present at Mr. Clinton's home**. Westinghouse designs nuclear reactors.

Wednesday, Mr. Clinton's spokesman, Ben Yarrow, issued what he called a ***"correction,"*** saying:

> ***"Today, Mr. Giustra told our office that in February 2007, he brought Mr. Dzhakishev***

from Kazatomprom to meet with President Clinton to discuss the future of nuclear energy."

Mr. Dzhakishev said he had a vivid memory of his Chappaqua visit, and a souvenir to prove it with a photograph of himself with the former president.

"I hung up the photograph of us and people asked me if I met with Clinton and I say, Yes, I met with Clinton," he said, smiling proudly.

The New York Times reports that the

"Monster deal stunned the mining industry, turning an unknown shell company into one of the world's largest uranium producers in a transaction ultimately worth tens of millions of dollars to Mr. Giustra."

THE RUSSIAN CONNECTION

One man who helped Giustra's *"UrAsia"* company get access to the Kazakhstan uranium deposits was named Sergey Kurzin. "Timing was everything," said Sergey Kurzin, a Russian-born businessman whose London-based company was brought into the deal by UrAsia because of his connections in Kazakhstan. Even with those connections, Mr. Kurzin said, it took four months to arrange a meeting with Kazatomprom. **Uranium One** is a uranium mining company founded in 1997 and owned by the Russian government with headquarters in Toronto and operations in Australia, Canada, Kazakhstan, South Africa and the United States. It is a Canadian corporation. **Rosatom State Energy Corporation**, a Russian State owned enterprise through a subsidiary, **ARMZ Uranium Holding** purchased 100% ownership in 2013. Let us review this. **Rosatom** owns **ARMZ**, which owns **Uranium One**. Thus, there are three levels of corporations between the Russian government and its wholly owned Uranium one. Now, let us look at **Uranium One's** history.

- The company was founded January 2, 1997 as *Southern Cross Resources Inc*.
  - Then on July 5, 2005, **Southern Cross Resources Inc**. and *Aflease* Gold and Uranium Resources Ltd announced that they would be merging under the name **SXR Uranium One Inc**.
    - In 2007, *Uranium One* acquired a controlling interest in *UrAsia Energy*, a Canadian firm with headquarters in Vancouver, from Frank Giustra.
    - *UrAsia Energy* has interests in rich uranium operations in Kazakhstan.
      - *UrAsia Energy's* acquisition of its Kazakhstan uranium interests from Kazatomprom followed a trip to Almaty in 2005 by Giustra and former U.S. President Bill Clinton where they met with Nursultan Nazarbayev, the leader of Kazakhstan. As noted previously, substantial contributions to the Clinton Foundation by Giustra followed.
    - In 2009, *ARMZ* acquired 16.6% of *Uranium One*. The deal was subject to anti-trust not finalized until the companies received Kazakh regulatory approvals, Canadian regulatory approvals and clearance from the US Committee on Foreign Investments as well as the Toronto and Johannesburg stock exchanges.
    - *ARMZ* took complete control of *Uranium One* in January 2013
      - *Uranium One* had 100% control of the *UrAsia Kazakhstan uranium mines*
      - *Uranium One* has 1/5th of U.S. Production of uranium. sApproval of the transfer to a Russian controlled state company occurred during Hillary

43

Clinton's Secretary of State Term of office.

A ***Uranium One*** sign that points to a 35,000-acre ranch owned by John Christensen, near the town of Gillette, Wyo. ***Uranium One*** has the mining rights to Mr. Christensen's property. [xv]

ARMZ took complete control of ***Uranium One*** in January 2013 in a transaction. In December 2013, an internal reorganization of Rosatom extinguished the interest of ***ARMZ*** making ***Uranium One*** a direct subsidiary of ***Rosatom***.

Approval of the transfer of American uranium resources to a Russian controlled- company occurred during Hillary Clinton's tenure as United States Secretary of State. There were a number of donations to the Clinton Foundation by principals of ***Uranium One*** as noted previously. During the same period there was a speaking engagement in Russia by former president Bill Clinton for which he was paid $500,000. No charges have yet been brought of a quid pro quo involving Bill or Hillary Clinton.

Did the above seem complex? It was designed that way. If everyone understood it then investigations would start on the Clintons. This is a very sophisticated deal where U.S. critical assets of uranium in the U.S. were transferred to the Russian Government.

CLINTON FOUNDATION AND GULF SHEIKS

Giustra met former US President <u>Bill Clinton</u> during fundraising efforts for tsunami relief in 2004. Giustra is a member of the board of trustees of the <u>Clinton Foundation</u>. Giustra provided his corporate jet for Clinton's fundraising campaign in Africa.

The governments and individuals donate money to the Clinton Giustra Enterprise Partnership who in turn bundles the donations to the Clinton Foundation. They could have donated directly to the Clinton Foundation.

However, these way sources of money are hidden and the money still moves to the Clinton Foundation. What do they get in return? This is hidden in the 30,000 removed private emails of Hillary Clinton.

WHO ARE SOME OF THE DONORS?

Governments that are controlled by Kings and dictators appear to be the principal donors. Richard Pollack of the Daily Caller [xvi] says that the Clintons received $100 million from Gulf Sheiks.

> *"These regimes are buying access. You have the Saudis. You have the Kuwaitis, Oman, Qatar and the UAE. There are massive conflicts of interest. It's beyond comprehension,"* Poole told The Daily Caller.

The article claims that the Clinton Foundation received at least $100 million from the monarchial Persian states. This could undermine Hillary's claim to carry out independent Middle East policies.

The benefits for Mideast oil producers amount to billions of dollars in oil trade, and as you might expect, Hillary Clinton is more than happy to oblige – at the expense of American energy companies and workers:

FRACKING

Fracking, or hydraulic fracturing, is forcing fractures in a rock layer, by fluid that is put under pressure. It can happen naturally, but it is now used to force oil and natural gas from shale.

In 2010, it was estimated that 60% of all new oil and gas wells worldwide were being hydraulically fractured. As of 2012, 2.5 million hydraulic fracturing jobs have been performed on oil and gas wells worldwide, more than one million of them in the United States.

The United States was heading toward energy independence and was beginning to ship oil out of the country because of Fracking. According to Jim Rickard, the Oil Sheiks in Saudi Arabia decided to put their competition out of business. They are doing so. It was simple for them. They have a wellhead cost of $1 to $10. The Frackers had costs above $60 / barrel. Most did not make money until it hit about $100 per barrel.

The Oil Sheiks just had to control the volume that they shipped. Yes, they are that big that they affect the world's oil price. Raise the volume means lower the price and Lower the volume means raise the price. They decided to keep the price of oil between $30 and $70 per barrel and have done so. The result is that frackers in America are going broke and declaring bankruptcy. They are currently in very bad economic shape.

Hillary's original position was to support the oil production from fracking. After the Clinton foundation received $100 million from the Mideast, she did a 180 and now she is against fracking. It is unclear what kind of promises the Clintons may have given the monarchs in return for their financial support. All we have is that the Clintons reversed their position after they received the $100 million. This was unveiled in the Presidential debate with Bernie Sanders. It is a policy position that puts her in alignment with the Oil Sheiks and opposed to the North American oil and gas fracking interests.

There is no plausible reason for why oil sheikhs in the Middle East would "donate" $100 million to The Clinton Foundation, save one. They believe that Hillary will receive a coronation as the President and they want access.

Indications are that the donation and then her flip-flop to support the policies of Mideast producers just months after the donations were made is evidence that she has been "paid to play".

Love him or hate him, Donald Trump's ***"Crooked Hillary"*** label sums her up precisely.

CONCLUSIONS

The Clinton fund, on its surface, turns out to be a sophisticated tax avoidance scheme. Its components are two charitable trusts. One is in Canada and the other is in the United States. The Canadian charitable trust is a partnership with a billionaire, Frank Giustra and Bill Clinton. The Canadian charity accepts contributions for the Clinton fund. They then bundled these contributions and send a single contribution to the Clinton fund. The original contribution is tax-free in Canada. The charitable contribution to the Clinton fund from the Canadian charity is also tax-free.

Given this operation, why don't the original contributors send their money directly to the Clinton fund? The answer is simple. They do not want their names known. In addition, the contributions allow plausible deniability on the part of the Clintons. By bundling the money in Canada and shipping single contributions to the Clinton bond, the donor names are dropped. Thus, large contributions can be made to Canada and passed on to the Clinton fund for use by the Clintons.

This is a form of money laundering. All money laundering focuses on source of funds and destination of funds. In this instance, the source of funds is billionaires, oil sheiks, third World governments and very rich individuals. One might think that these are just charitable contributions. However, some contributions have hit $100 million. In this large contribution spectrum, the originator usually wants something in return. In this instance, it is probably access to Bill or Hillary Clinton. If the Clintons are in office, then the contributions go up.

We examined two transactions in this book. One was for a uranium mining operation in Kazakhstan and in the U.S. and another was to stop oil tracking in this country.

Frank Giustra instituted the uranium mining operation with UrAsia after Bill Clinton introduced him to the president of Kazakhstan. Within two days, Frank Giustra received a contract that allowed him to mine if he paid a royalty of $450 million. He owned an unknown shell company that was called UrAsia. As soon as that contract was completed by paying the $450 million in December, Bill Clinton received a $151 million contribution from Giustra for the

47

Clinton fund. The net of this transaction is that Frank Giustra sold his company to Uranium One and they sold their company to MRZ, which was eventually bought by Rostrum, the wholly owned Russian State firm that owned 100% of MRZ corp. Thus, all the UrAsia uranium mining in Kazakhstan and 20% of the uranium mining in the United States is now controlled by Rostrum – a nationalized Russian firm.

The interesting fact is that Hillary Clinton as Secretary of the State approved this transaction before she left office. After the transaction was completed, the Clinton foundation collected $151 million in contributions.

The second area of interest that was affected by Hillary Clinton is fracking. Initially Hillary Clinton was a hundred percent for any fracking in this country. However, the Clinton fund received $100 million as a donation to the Clinton fund from the oil sheiks in the Mideast. As soon as the money was in the Clinton fund, she switched sides and promptly changed her position and is now anti-fracking with her comments and support.

Jim Rickards reports that with respect to fracking, the oil sheiks about three years ago decided to put the oil producers who use fracture, their competition, out of business.

They have been successful. Most are going bankrupt.

Jim Rickard reports that it works like this. Saudi Arabia has a wellhead cost of producing a barrel of oil somewhere between $1 and $10. The frackers need $60-$100 to be profitable. Saudi Arabia oil fields are large enough to control the world price in oil. When they want a lower price, they opened the spigot. If they want a higher price, they close the spigot. They decided to maintain the price of oil in a $30-$70 range for years if necessary to put the frackers out of business. They have accomplished this over the last few years.

It is clear to me after reviewing what happened in the uranium example as well is in the fracking example that the Clintons are in a "pay to play" team where they must be paid to use their influence to accomplish something for the donators. They use the Clinton fund to take in tax-free "pay" to play for their expenses. They have 2,000 people at work around the world. The highly visible ones will come with Hillary if she wins the Presidency.

Is this legal? The FBI is currently investigating that question. They only do criminal investigations. Thus, the FBI has a criminal investigation focused on the Clinton Fund.

I have no idea what they will conclude now that I have seen the results of what Comey concluded on the security of national classified assets. She is and was clearly guilty multiple times but he gave her freedom because it was not her intent that is not mentioned in the law.

What to Do? After writing this book, I contacted an old friend, Col. John Stevens, who has spent 30 years in intelligence for this nation. I asked what he thought of Hillary's actions with the Server. He sent me his views which <u>he had done independently</u> since he had not read the text as yet. Upon reading it, I immediately asked him if I could publish it as APPENDIX A, THE CLINTON INDICTMENT. I found it was perfect for the ending of this book. I too believe that Hillary should be indicted.

I believe that if Hillary went into any office, especially the Presidency, it would be dangerous for this nation. Her actions clearly show that she believes that she is above the law and regards actions that would potentially harm this country as secondary if she can make money at it doing it. One instance, is the uranium deal with Russia. Examine Appendix A and think about it.

APPENDIX A

THE CLINTON INDICTMENT

Col. John Stevens

"John Stevens is a retired Army Lieutenant Colonel, with an in-depth background in Signal Intelligence. He currently resides in Northern Virginia."

The Charge:

Hillary Rodham Clinton, former First Lady of the United States, former Senator from the State of New York, former Secretary of State of the United States, and current Democrat Party candidate of the presidency of the United States, is accused of willfully and deliberately taking actions that violated criminal segments of the US Code relating to national security. In doing so, she placed numerous selected elements of United States policies and defense matter in jeopardy to the extent of exceptionally grave danger.

The Specifications:

1. Clinton did, in 2008, on being named the presumptive Secretary of State, take action to establish an email server and capability not of government provision and not in a government facility.
2. Clinton did, by her own admission, use the illicit non-government email capability during the total period of her tenure as Secretary of State.
3. Clinton did, by her own admission, use the illicit capability to send and receive more than fifty thousand (50,000) emails during her tenure as Secretary of State. Subsequent revelations indicate that this traffic contained a mix of both classified and non-classified materials.

4. Clinton did, by her own admission, and subsequent to her tenure as Secretary of States, turn over to the Department of State more the twenty thousand (20,000) printout of emails which **Clinton**, and her staff allegedly, deemed as official business, as thus as official records.

5. Clinton did, by her own admission; attempt to erase from the illicit server thirty thousand (30,000) emails, which she, and allegedly her staff, deemed as personal and not within the government's interests.

6. Clinton has continually in public stated that there was nothing marked as classified material in any of her email traffic on the illicit server.

The Case:

1. With respect to Specification 1. It is not clear whether Clinton had discussed the use of an external server with the State Department security and information technology personnel. It is presumed she did not. Clinton's actions were taken to avoid the legal provisions of federal records keeping and freedom of information request responses, but this cannot be proven with information currently available. The Specification is only useful as the launching point for the subsequent alleged criminal actions.

2. With respect to Specification 2. This again sets the stage for Clinton's admission of criminal actions involving the use of emails and the Internet.

3. With respect to Specification 3. Clinton did presumably (and possibly provably) put the nation at risk by the obvious and intense use of the illicit email system. In her position, the foreign and domestic intelligence activities have a more than casual interest in the easily identifiable and unprotected email correspondence of the Secretary of State of the United States. Since, in order to assume the position as Secretary, Clinton would have had to be subject to several briefings on security matters and therefore sign numerous security non-disclosure forms with respect to the programs she would then be granted access to, she cannot, for an instant, be assumed naive of the security risk her unprotected emails presented.

Having such knowledge and then using the unsafe means of email communications constitutes deliberate gross negligence on Clinton's part. Further, Clinton had to have had some semblance of knowledge that the activity she was executing was in fact unlawful. Both actions are criminal under the provisions of 18 US Code, Section 793, subsections (f) (1) and (2). Clinton is, **by her own admission, guilty of this offense**

4. With respect to Specification 4. Clinton turned over 22,000 email printed pages to the State Department more than a year subsequent to the closure of her tenure as Secretary of State. The department review, deliberately slowed by the provision of paper, vice electronic media, revealed that more than two thousand (2000) of the provided emails contained classified material, in contrast to Clinton's numerous statements to the contrary.

5. In fact, twenty two (22) of the emails were judged to be of TOP SECRET, or special compartmented information security classification; none were originated in the State Department. Each occurrence of the TOP SECRET materials is a violation of Section 793, subsections (f) (1) and (2), and each, especially the compartmented information, must be charged individually as such.

6. In addition, at least one email exchange made public depicts Clinton's staff noting that an information note was classified; Clinton directed her staff to make it a "non-paper", i.e. remove the classification markings, and send it to her on the illicit unsecured email system. **This collective action is a violation of US Code, Section 793, subsection (g) initially, as well as a violation of US Code, Section 1924 in its entirety, and a violation of US Code, Section 2071, subsection (b).** In short, Clinton and her staff are totally and completely guilty of collusion, deliberate and willful intent to circumvent security regulations and intent, and deliberate and willful intent to mishandle official documents within the security system.

7. With respect to Specification 5. Clinton allegedly cleared the illicit server of thirty thousand (30,000) emails, noting that they were not of government concern; they were alleged

to pertain to family activities, yoga, etc. This is viewed skeptically, for the period involved corresponded to massive dealings of foreign nations and interests with respect to the Clinton Foundation. The possibility of additional security violations exist, as well as massive collusion and corruption between the State Department, foreign governments and interests, and the Clinton Foundation. Note: The FBI has seized the illicit server and is apparently working to retrieve the cleared content of its memories. Should such action reveal anything, the FBI will determine subsequent action.

8. With respect to Specification 6. Clinton's public statements have the appearance of a carefully calculated campaign to defuse any interest in her illicit emails. It is interesting to note the very careful wording of every utterance concerning the subject by Clinton; there are no direct statements pertaining to the content of her emails.

A Summary

It is self-evident, from Clinton's own admissions, that illegal acts with respect to the handling of national security information were conducted. These acts were apparently conducted during the entirety of her tenure as Secretary of State of the United States of America. Furthermore, it appears that Clinton and her staff were involved in deliberate conspiracy to conduct such acts and to keep the acts concealed from proper authority.

From the evidence yet publically revealed, Clinton deliberately mishandled twenty two (22) **TOP SECRET** information items in email form, thus putting the nation into exceptionally grave danger. This has recently been confirmed by the apprehension of a Romanian hacker, who has admitted hacking the Clinton email complex at least twice, noting that doing so was "easy". One can assume that more sophisticated organizations, say the intelligence activities of China, Israel, and Russia, did so, and exploited the source on a constant basis.

The Federal Bureau of Investigation (FBI) has obtained the physical assets of Clinton's server and the individual who created the server installation and performed servicing and maintenance thereon. This individual has been given immunity from criminal prosecution in exchange for detailed knowledge of events relating to Clinton's server. The combination of FBI technical skills at retrieving data from "erased" data storage elements, and the debriefing of the Clinton technician should create a strong case for the prosecution of Clinton as a violator of national security laws, in both the letter and the intent.

It should be obvious to the most casual observer that Clinton and her associates, yet to be named, are guilty of massive security violations, and the derogation of the trust of the nation. They must be indicted and brought to trial for these and other such other actions as related thereto. Failure to indict such conduct by the Department of Justice and the Attorney General is a self-evident cause for impeachment proceedings. While awkward politically, the indictment of a former First Lady, a former Senator, and a former Secretary of State must be done to prove no one in the United States of America is above the law in any capacity.

Appenix A – US Code

U.S. Code: Title 18 - CRIMES AND CRIMINAL PROCEDURE

18 U.S. Code § 793 - Gathering, transmitting or losing defense information (extracted)

(f) **Whoever, being entrusted with** or having lawful possession or control of **any document**, writing, code book, signal book, sketch, photograph, photographic negative, blueprint, plan, map, model, instrument, appliance, note, or information, relating to the national defense, (1) **through gross negligence** permits the same to be removed from its proper place of custody or delivered to anyone in violation of his trust, or to be lost, stolen, **abstracted**, or destroyed, or (2) **having knowledge that the same has been illegally removed** from its proper place of custody or delivered to anyone in violation of its trust, or lost, or stolen, abstracted, or destroyed, and **fails to make prompt report** of such loss, theft, abstraction, or destruction to his superior officer— Shall be fined under this title or imprisoned not more than ten years, or both.

(g) **If two or more persons conspire to violate any of the foregoing provisions of this section,** and **one or more of**

such persons do any act to effect the object of the conspiracy, **each of the parties to such conspiracy shall be subject to the punishment** provided for the offense, which is the object of such conspiracy.

18 U.S. Code § 1924 - Unauthorized removal and retention of classified documents or material

Whoever, being an officer, employee, contractor, or consultant of the United States, and, by virtue of his office, employment, position, or contract, **becomes possessed** of documents or materials containing classified information of the United States, **knowingly removes such documents or materials without authority** and **the intent to retain such documents or materials at an unauthorized location** shall be fined under this title or imprisoned for not more than one year, or both.

(b)   For purposes of this section, the provision of documents and materials to the Congress shall not constitute an offense under subsection (a).

(c)   In this section, the term "classified information of the United States" means information originated, owned, or possessed by the United States Government **concerning the national defense or foreign** relations of the United States that has been **determined pursuant to law or Executive order** to require protection against unauthorized disclosure in the interests of national security.

18 U.S. Code 2071 - Concealment, removal, or mutilation generally

(a)   Whoever willfully and unlawfully conceals, removes, mutilates, obliterates, or destroys, or attempts to do so, or, with intent to do so takes and carries away any record, proceeding, map, book, paper, document, or other thing, filed or deposited with any clerk or officer of any court of the United States, or in any public office, or with any judicial or public officer of the United States, shall be fined under this title or imprisoned not more than three years, or both.

(b) **Whoever, having the custody of any** such record, proceeding, map, book, document, paper, or **other thing, willfully and unlawfully conceals, removes, mutilates, obliterates, falsifies, or destroys the same,** shall be fined under this title or imprisoned not more than three years, or both; **and shall forfeit his office and <u>be disqualified from holding any office under the United States</u>.** As used in this subsection, the term "office" does not include the office held by any person as a retired officer of the Armed Forces of the United States.

Visit: www.Ravengeopolnews.com/ebooks

LIST OF REFERENCES

i _**Office of the Secretary: Evaluation of Email Records Management and Cybersecurity Requirements, ESP-15-03. Office of Evaluation and Special Projects, OIG Office of Inspector General U.S. Department of State*Broadcasting Board of Governors**_, May 2016, pp.1-79.

ii Ibid, OIG, p.5.

iii Ibid, OIG, p.59.

iv Michael Hayden, "Hillary Clinton's Continuing Email Scandal", _**Special Report Judicial Watch**_, p.11.

v Ibid, Joseph DiGenova, p.11.

vi Ibid, p.10.

vii Ibid, Joseph DiGenova, p.22.

viii Ibid., Judge Lamberth

ix Ibid, Judge Sullivan, p. 25.

x Tom Fitton, _**The Judicial Watch Verdict**_, June 2016, p.4.

xi James Comey, _**"FBI: Clinton 'Careless', Not 'Criminal'"**_, **Wall Street Journal**, p.1.

xii are all and

xiii Ben Shapiro, _**"Hillary Clinton's Long History of Hiding Documents"**_, Breitbart, March 4 2015 xiv Richard Pollack, ***"Exclusive: Persian Gulf Sheiks Gave Bill and Hillary $100 Million", Daily Caller,*** May 11, 2016

xv Mathew Staver NY Times (Photo), Jo Becker and Mike McIntire, ***"Cash Flowed to Clinton Foundation During the Russian Uranium Deal",*** NY Times, April 23 2015

xvi Ibid, Pollac